Double Genesis

Double Genesis

Locke, Jesus,

& American Populism

Eric Leif Davin

DavinBooks
P.O. Box 90087
Pittsburgh, PA 15224

Double Genesis

Locke, Jesus,
& American Populism

ISBN 978-1-387-48240-5

Dedication:

For True Believers

Introduction

The American Socialist Party, led by Eugene V. Debs, was founded in 1901. For a brief time it seemed to promise the possibility of growing into a mass movement. However, unlike in Europe, socialism never became an enduring and truly mass political movement in America.

Thus, as early as 1906, German economist and sociologist Werner Sombart was able to publish a book asking his famous question about American political exceptionalism, *Why Is There No Socialism in the United States?* Sombart's answer was, basically, "roast beef and apple pie." Under the assumption, common to Marx and Marxists, and perhaps most others, that material deprivation and desperation alone are what drive people to revolt, Sombart declared that Americans were never deprived and desperate enough. Widespread American material prosperity, he concluded, meant Americans were never truly susceptible to socialism.[1]

Commentators of a certain political persuasion have been attempting to provide their own answers to Sombart's question ever since. I do not

---

[1]If deprivation and desperation were what drive people to revolt, the entire history of humanity would be one long history of revolts. Instead, revolts are exceedingly rare responses by desperate people, and those that do occur are closely studied to discover why they happened.

intend to go into a long historiographical rendition of their answers. To my mind, none of them have been fully persuasive.

But, the fact remains that, more than a century after Sombart asked his question, America still does not have a mass socialist movement. I believe the answer lies in the fact that Americans were, and are, already deeply committed to another political ideology.

This other political ideology is inhaled in the air we breathe and, through a process of osmosis, has claimed our hearts and minds from our very founding as a society. All widespread political dissent in America is expressed in the language of this ideology, precluding the possibility of a rival ideology of dissent, such as socialism, from gaining a mass following. Regardless of the economic realities, it does not view America as a society stratified by economic classes, as socialism does, of a working class and a capitalist class. Instead, it thinks of America as a basically "classless" society.

This is why Americans are so befuddled if you ask them which economic class they belong to. We don't think in those terms. Thus, after struggling with the question, Americans will usually, eventually, reply that they are "middle-class." Isn't America, they will say, basically a middle-class society?

Oh, they will concede there are the rich and famous. But, those are a tiny minority. And there are the truly poor, another minority. But Americans, even those who are struggling financially, will say that they, and the vast bulk of Americans, are middle-class. Most of us, they believe, are all in the same boat. Even dissident movements reflect this belief when they say that, "We are the 99% vs. the 1%."

Sometimes we say that this belief is the belief in democracy, that democracy is the basis of our national identity. But, democracy can take many institutional forms, and America's national belief is more specific than that. In fact, the basis of it is something seldom mentioned, and when it is mentioned, it is usually mentioned in a negative light. Put simply, populism America's basic political belief, and is the basis of the American identity.

It is curious that Werner Sombart, an otherwise insightful sociologist, overlooked this possible answer to his question, as it was hiding in plain sight. Sombart published his book merely a few years after the political fluorescence of the most successful third party in American history (excepting, perhaps, the Republican Party). This was the People's Party, a party that swept through large swaths of America in the 1890s, electing hundreds of candidates to all levels of office, including state governors and members of Congress. Yet, somehow, Sombart missed it – and the political ideology it espoused.

The People's Party is usually better known by its unofficial name, the "Populist Party," and its political ideology is called, therefore, "populism." This is an ideology that champions the great mass of the undifferentiated "people" versus the handful of elites. And, despite the rise and fall of the Populist Party, it is the political ideology that dominated the hearts and minds of Americans before the appearance of the party, and continues, to this day, to dominate the hearts and minds of Americans. Because of this dominance, there was no room in the hearts and minds of Americans for the rival political ideology of socialism. America already had its political ideology.

But, if this was the American ideology from

our very founding, where did it come from? What was its genesis?

Actually, I believe there was a double genesis. One of those was classical liberal republicanism, growing out of the writings of European Enlightenment thinkers such as John Locke. This genesis, in fact, is the one most commonly cited when political commentators discuss the genesis of the American polity. And, so far as the rational and theoretical foundations of the Constitution and the particulars of our system of government go, this is true. When pushed to explicate the American polity, Americans will usually begin to speak in the language of classical liberal republicanism.

But, there was also another, simultaneous, and complementary genesis, closer to the hearts and minds of ordinary Americans. This was the Christian tradition, the Protestant tradition, a tradition of hostility to "antichristian" hierarchy and elites and an emphasis upon the general equality of true believers living in a community of saints.

In other words, America had two parents. One was the European Enlightenment. The other was Christianity. In Europe, these two parents seemed to always be hostile to each other. They seemed to be irrevocably incompatible. But, in America, a strange alchemy took place, and they became wedded in an embrace that formed our national identity.

Today, we would perhaps not speak of this other, religious, genesis of our national identity in an explicitly religious language, as we live in a more secular age. But the identity that grew out of the wedding of these two parents is nevertheless the child of this strange double genesis.

Power to the People

After Donald Trump's presidential victory in 2016, populism suffered a lot of abuse at the hands of political pundits and Sunday morning talk show hosts. A prominent critic was Fareed Zakaria, a *Washington Post* columnist and sometime essayist for *TIME*. Zakaria's first most visible attack on populism was an article titled, "Populism on the March: Why the West is in Trouble," in the November-December, 2016, issue of *Foreign Affairs*. The title tells it all.

This fear and distrust of populism among the elites has a long history, going back at the very least to the 1950s, when liberal intellectuals decried the demagoguery of Senator Joseph McCarthy. But what all these media commentators seemingly failed to understand was that populism is not a strange aberration of democracy that rears its ugly head during times of crisis. Broadly speaking, populism is the belief that the will of the people should prevail over the will of privileged elites. Thus, populism is the concept of democracy itself, and elite fears of populism are actually fears of democracy.

This fear of democracy has a tradition in this country that goes back to our founding as a nation when the Founders wrote the Constitution, and all its strictures and "balance of powers," to curtail what they saw as the dangers of too much democracy.

(For just two examples: There was the Senate, through which all legislation had to pass. Originally, no voter could vote for the Senate. State legislators chose Senators, and the explicit purpose of the Senate was to stymie any unwise laws that might arise from the popularly elected House. And, should unwise legislation somehow pass even the Senate, there was the Supreme Court, where wise judges, installed by the Senate and serving for life, could overrule the legislation as… "Unconstitutional.")

Nor is populism the monolithic political philosophy these commentators fearfully portrayed. It can indeed be manifested as what might be called "Right Populism." Would-be dictator Donald Trump, and other demagogues like him around the world who have historically exploited it to ride to power, exemplify this version of populism. This type of anti-democratic populism is well documented, and it is this version of populism that these pundits fear and decry.

But populism is a double-sided coin, and it can also be manifested as a radically democratic "Left Populism." Both versions are powerful. In the United States, for example, Senator Bernie Sanders comes to mind as exemplifying this more democratic Left Populism. In the 2016 presidential primaries, Donald Trump garnered 13.3 million votes of Republican voters with his version of Right Populism. But Bernie Sanders garnered almost as many Democratic primary votes, 13 million, with his version of a Left Populism that promised "A Future To Believe In." Further, he won 22 states, including states that Hillary Clinton lost to Trump in the general election, such as Indiana, Wisconsin, and Michigan.

Left Populism is a protest tradition, one that champions the common people against the rich and powerful, that has always been America's dominant ideology of dissent. Most American radicals in our history, including working class radicals, have commonly thought of themselves as "the people" instead of "the workers," even though they may have been of the working class. Given the dominance of Left Populism in American protest thought, it should surprise no one that the all-time best-selling history of American radicalism, with well over one million copies in print, celebrates America's Left Populist heritage. It is, of course, Howard Zinn's *A People's History of the United States*. Zinn's title, and the thrust of his book, helps explain why it is so popular.

Before the radical upsurge of the 1960s, the other great period of twentieth century protest was the 1930s. Despite what the Left might wish to believe about the legendary labor upheavals of the 1930s, it was Left Populism, not some variant of Marxism, that mobilized "the workers" in that earlier period of radicalism. Indeed, the labor struggles of the Thirties were part of a wider Left Populist movement at that time for inclusion of the downtrodden in the American Dream. This is why they rallied to President Franklin D. Roosevelt and made the Democratic Party the majority party in the New Deal Era. Journalist Bill Moyers recalls that FDR seemed to be the champion of all the "Forgotten Men" who were "Lost in America," the entire dispossessed and tossed aside.

Bill Moyers was raised a Baptist in East Texas where his father had left school after the fourth grade to begin life as a cotton picker. His father bought a radio with his meager savings just so he could listen to FDR, "the aristocrat speaking up for common people," during his "Fireside Chats."

And the message of FDR and his New Deal, said Moyers, the message his father heard coming over that radio in the East Texas cotton fields was this: "Class and power were not fixed by Nature; inequality was wrong and unemployment humiliating; runaway capitalism could be tamed, privilege checked, monopolies broken up, an end put to government by organized money. Roosevelt talked of democracy to people down and out, broken and feeling betrayed. He made them think they had a stake in it and a responsibility for it."[2]

The common people Moyers spoke of embodied a down-to-earth, blue collar, multi-ethnic, populist ideal we find elsewhere in popular culture during the Thirties. This ideal is found, for instance, in the thousands of photos taken by the photographers sent out across America by the Farm Security Administration (FSA). From 1935 to 1943 Roy Stryker directed a team of some twenty FSA photographers who produced over 270,000 pictures of America's "common people." Stryker's photographers took some of the iconic images we have of the Great Depression, such as Dorothea Lange's "Okie Madonna," broken down somewhere in a California farm field with her children hanging on her.

The reason these photos are so populist is because Roy Stryker deliberately sought pictures of "the common people," the hard working survivors who built America. "I think it's significant," Stryker later said, "that in our entire collection we have only one picture of Franklin Roosevelt, the most newsworthy man of the era – this, mind you, in a collection that's sometimes said to have reported the feel and smell and taste of the Thirties even more

---

[2]Commentary by Bill Moyers on the NBC Evening News, April 11, 1995, commemorating the 50th anniversary of Roosevelt's death on April 12th, 1945.

vividly than the news media.... you'll find no record of big people or big events in the collection.... not a single shot of Wall Street, and absolutely no celebrities."[3]

This ideal was in the air. In 1936, in what he termed his own favorite poem, Carl Sandburg celebrated "The People, Yes!"[4] In 1941, Pulitzer Prize-winning poet Stephen Vincent Benet urged us to "Listen To The People." These people included, "Paul Bunchick and the Greek who runs the Greek's/ The black-eyed children out of Sicily/ All of them there and all of them a nation. / Our voice is not one voice, but many voices. / Not one man's, not the greatest, but the people's."[5]

In 1942 Aaron Copeland wrote a hymn of praise to "the common man" in his "Lincoln Portrait," the most stirring portion of which is his triumphant beginning, the "Fanfare for the Common Man." Copeland has a reader quote passages from Abraham Lincoln to the accompaniment of stirring music, passages such as "The spirit of slavery is the same as the spirit that says, 'You work and toil and earn bread, and I'll eat it.' No matter in what shape it comes,

---

[3]Roy Emerson Stryker and Nancy Wood, *In This Proud Land: America 1935-1943 as Seen in the FSA Photographs*, Galahad Books: New York, 1973, p. 8.

[4]Carl Sandburg, "The People, Yes," in *The American Tradition in Literature, Vol. 2*, edited by Sculley Bradley, Richmond Croom Beatty, and E. Hudson Long, W.W. Norton & Co.: New York, 1956, pp. 960, 962.

[5]Stephen Vincent Benet, "Listen to the People, Independence Day, 1941," in *The Stephen Vincent Benet Pocket Book*, edited by Robert Van Gelder, Pocket Books: New York, 1946, pp. 367, 379.

whether from a mouth of a king, or from one race of men as an apology for enslaving another race, it is the same tyrannical principle."

This was a theme also commonly expressed by radical labor unions in the Thirties, such as the Independent Textile Union of Rhode Island, which had approvingly published the very same Lincoln passage five years before in a 1937 issue of its newspaper.[6]

But perhaps the musical genre that most closely reflected the spirit of the times was folk music. Americans have long composed and sung "traditional" songs such as cowboy laments, Delta blues, Kentucky bluegrass, and the hillbilly songs of Appalachia, with their roots in Elizabethan and Scots-Irish ballads. It was not until the twentieth century, however, that such songs came to be identified as "folk songs" of "the people," a populist musical genre that cohered in the 1930s. And it is no accident that the music we most closely identify with the Thirties is folk music, a genre which describes the lives, loves, and labors of the common people.

It is also no accident, then, that the two periods that witnessed the proliferation of folk songs, the Thirties and the Sixties, were also the only two eras of the twentieth century that witnessed the emergence and flowering of significant populist and oppositional counter-cultures.

Even the obdurate Communist Party eventually adopted the Left Populism of the times with its 1935 "Popular Front" strategy. That year the party changed its official slogan to, "Communism is Twentieth Century Americanism." Meanwhile, the

---

[6] *ITU News*, May, 1937, p. 5.

volunteers it sent to fight in Spain against the fascists in that country's civil war did so as members of "The Abraham Lincoln Brigade."

At the same time, the Communist-affiliated Composers Collective began including in its *Workers Song Books* indigenous folk music of all types, including songs of farmers, miners, urban workers, and African-Americans – songs of "the people." It should come as no surprise, therefore, that the Communist Party reached its most influence and its highest membership levels during this Popular Front period when it promoted Left Populism.

The most influential folk singer of the Thirties was no doubt Woody Guthrie. He was born into an impoverished Oklahoma dust bowl family and was closely associated with the Communist Party. Guthrie composed more than a thousand songs reflecting the decade's spirit of Left Populist protest. Perhaps his most well known song is "This Land is Your Land," which declared, "this land belongs to you and me," not, it suggested, to the rich and the corporations.

In 1941 Guthrie joined Pete Seeger, Lee Hays, and others to form the Almanac Singers, a popular folk group that sang for C.I.O. (Congress of Industrial Organizations) organizing campaigns and political rallies. After World War II, as America became more politically conservative, Guthrie, Seeger, and other members of the Almanac Singers kept the Left Populist spirit of folk music alive through such groups as People's Songs. It was at a meeting of the People's Songs Board of Directors that Pete Seeger and Lee Hays wrote "If I Had a Hammer," a song that gained widespread popularity in the early Sixties after the folk trio of Peter, Paul, and Mary made it a hit. In the song, Seeger and Hays proclaimed that they would hammer out justice and freedom “all over this land.”

This Left Populist theme was also echoed in the films of Italian director Frank Capra, perhaps the most popular and successful film director of the 1930s, responsible for such films as “Mr. Smith Goes To Washington” and “Meet John Doe,” both of which reflected a Left Populist point of view.

Born in Sicily in 1897, Capra immigrated to Los Angeles with his parents in 1903. When America entered World War I, he joined the army. After the Armistice, Capra returned to Los Angeles, but was unable to find a job. He bummed around for several years, working at odd jobs, ending up down and out in San Francisco. It was during those days that Capra came to believe that, "The rich have it all, but accomplish little."[7]

The essence of Frank Capra's Left Populism, reflected in his subsequent films, was that it was the decent, hard-working, "little guy" who really represented all that was most American – while the wealthy and the representatives of the powerful represented a venal corruption of the American ideal. This worldview meshed with what most Americans believed, and that was what made them so popular.

Populism, then, has always been the dominant ideology of dissent in America – because it is the way most Americans view the political world.

---

[7]Jimmie Hicks, “Frank Capra,” *Films in Review*, September-October 1992, p. 291.

All Men Are Created Equal

The source of this ideology, as I have said, has a double genesis. On the one hand, it derives from a secularization of a religious tradition that has a deep past. On the other, more well known and more often cited, it derives from the rationalist European Enlightenment tradition of John Locke's liberal republicanism.

The ideology of liberal republicanism asserts certain things. For example, in the Declaration of Independence of 1776, Thomas Jefferson stated that it was a "self evident truth" that "all men are created equal and endowed by their Creator with certain unalienable rights," the chief among them being "life, liberty, and the pursuit of happiness."

The "self evident truth" that all men were born free and equal was not original to Jefferson. Indeed, he acknowledged his intellectual debt to Enlightenment thinkers who came before him, most importantly English theorist John Locke.

In his 1690 *Essay Concerning the True Original Extent and End of Civil Government,* written to justify the new constitutional monarchy established in England by the Glorious Revolution of 1688, Locke laid down the principles of Jefferson's Declaration. In this essay, Locke elaborated his concept of limited government based on the consent of the governed. His starting point, however, was a primitive state of nature comprised of free and equal individuals. The "law of nature," therefore, entitled all individuals equally to life, liberty, and property (the latter of which Jefferson transformed into "the pursuit of happiness").

However, by a social contract they delegated the administration of this law of nature to government, while retaining the inherent rights to freedom and equality that, not their "Creator," but the "law of nature" gave them. Jefferson embedded not only Locke's doctrines, but also his very phrases into the Declaration of Independence. By doing so, however, he was simply stating what most Americans already believed. The New World of America, it seemed to them, was the very embodiment of Locke's original "state of nature." Indeed, Locke himself had once written, in his *Second Treatise on Civil Government*, that, "In the beginning, all the world was America..." Further, beginning with the Mayflower Compact of 1620, he said, those coming to America from Europe had traditionally written social contracts establishing a form of government agreed to by free and equal property owners. Thus, historian Louis Hartz famously pointed out in 1955 in his *The Liberal Tradition in America,* "Locke dominates American political thought, as no thinker anywhere dominates the political thought of a nation. He is a massive national cliché."[8]

Hartz went on to note that America had never experienced feudalism, nor did it have a titled aristocracy. And, with the triumph of the Revolution, it no longer had a king, nor any serious political tendency defending monarchism. The "common man"

---

[8]Louis Hartz, *The Liberal Tradition in America*, Harcourt, Brace & World: New York, 1955,
p. 140.

may not have thought of politics in the specific language of Locke, but everyone believed in a limited government based upon the consent of free and equal individuals. Thus, all political debate took place within that narrow range of ideas of limited government and equal rights to property ownership, that is, "the pursuit of happiness." "Catastrophes have not been able to destroy" the idea, Hartz argued, "proletariats have refused to give it up."[9] Hence, "In...the Jeffersonian and Jacksonian eras...virtually everyone, including the nascent industrial worker, has the mentality of the independent entrepreneur."[10]

Such beliefs were based on a fair amount of reality, the general material comfort Sombart pointed to. While America was not Thomas Jefferson's idealized yeoman Eden, an analysis of the 1798 land tax figures reveals that 52% of the free white males were farmers who owned their own land. Thus, they were economically independent and participated in political discourse as socio-economic equals at a time when property ownership was a prerequisite for being a voter. This was no doubt the highest percentage of land-owning "citizens" in the world at that time. Not only was there more equality in 1800 among free white males than anywhere else, there was also probably more equality in America for this population than there ever would be again. Further, there was the hope and expectation that landless free white males would eventually move up to become landowners themselves.

---

[9]Hartz, p. 62.
[10]Hartz, p. 89.

It should come as no surprise, therefore, to discover that the labor literature of the age was saturated with the idea of yeoman free holding and, "During the Jacksonian era...labor writers were clinging to Jefferson's small propertied individualism.... Jefferson emphasized the concrete fact of the ownership of property, which to be sure was not a characteristic of the industrial worker. But...liberalism...was largely a psychological matter, a product of the spirit of Locke...[that] could infect the factory as well as it infected the land."[11]

Even in the 1830s, however, Americans were already feeling the strains and tensions resulting from the centralizing and monopolizing tendencies of a developing industrial capitalism. Their deep-rooted belief in liberal republicanism informed their attitudes toward the emerging new order. Thus, historian Herbert Gutman tells us, "workers transformed the political, social, and economic beliefs and practices they carried from the American Revolution into a distinctive critique of early American capitalism. Central to these beliefs and practices was republicanism. The transformation of American men and women into dependent wage earners in the years before 1840 tested not only their adaptability to specialized labor, but also the appropriateness of their republican ideology.... 'Give a man power over my subsistence,' Alexander Hamilton had warned, 'and he has a right to my whole moral body.' Hamilton and his generation did not live into the early industrial capitalist era, but republican ideology survived them

[11]Hartz, pp. 123, 122.

and gained a new life among the artisans and laborers of industrializing America."[12]

This same fundamental belief in Lockian liberalism, the belief in liberty, equality, and the inherent right to own property, was at the heart of the Free Soil movement of the 1840s and resulted in the birth of the Republican Party in the 1850s. By then, however, the generalized Lockian ideal had acquired a specific name: Free Labor. It was a concept, Eric Foner tells us in his seminal work, *Free Soil, Free Labor, Free Men,* that was "the heart of the Republican ideology, and expressed a coherent social outlook, a model of the good society... For Republicans, 'free labor' meant labor with economic choices, with the opportunity to quit the wage-earning class. A man who remained all his life dependent on wages for his livelihood appeared almost as unfree as the southern slave."[13]

President Abraham Lincoln reflected this Lockian free labor ideal in 1861 at the beginning of the Civil War, placing that war in context. A slave was a slave forever, he said, but in the North, there was "no such...thing as a free man being fixed for life in the condition of a hired laborer.... Men, with their families...work for themselves on their farms, in their houses, and in their shops, taking the whole product for themselves, and asking no favors of capital on the

---

[12]Herbert Gutman, *Power and Culture: Essays on The American Working Class,* edited by Ira Berlin, Pantheon Books: New York, 1987, p. 381.

[13]Eric Foner, *Free Soil, Free Labor, Free Men: The Ideology of the Republican Party Before the Civil War,* Oxford University Press: New York, 1970, pp. 11, 16-17.

one hand nor of hired laborers or slaves on the other."[14]

Northern farmers and workers were, in this view of the ideal society, essentially economically self-sufficient middle class small businessmen or, if they were not at present, hoped soon to become so. It was this concept of an ideal society of free small property owners that lay behind the plans of some Radical Republicans after the war to break up the large antebellum southern plantations and redistribute the land to the ex-slaves. With the right to vote and "forty acres and a mule" the ex-slaves would have both democratic and economic freedom and equality, and would thus be able to defend their rights in the postbellum southern world.

In fact, Eric Foner says, "The Republicans' enmity toward the South was intimately bound up with their loyalty to the society of small-scale capitalism of essentially equal citizens that they perceived in the North. It was its identification with the aspirations of the farmers, small entrepreneurs, and craftsmen of northern society that gave the Republican ideology much of its dynamic, progressive, and optimistic quality. Yet, paradoxically, at the same time of its greatest success, the seeds of a later failure of that ideology were already present. Fundamental changes were at work in the social and economic structure of the North, transforming and undermining many of its free labor assumptions."[15]

---

[14]Foner, p. 29.
[15]Foner, pp. 316-317.

In the years after the Civil War, the ideal of basic economic equality continued to be widely held, but it was already becoming increasingly unlikely that an industrial worker or a farm laborer would ever achieve economic independence.

It was this conflict between old ideals and new realities that generated the endemic and increasing social conflict in the North. Thus, as David Montgomery demonstrated in his path breaking 1967 book, *Beyond Equality,* the liberal republican ideology of equality motivated workers' movements in the North to raise fundamental challenges to industrial capitalism during both the Civil War and the subsequent Reconstruction years.[16] Because of their ideology, workers believed a good society was one of "haves and will-haves." And, they believed, that was what America, the land of equal opportunity, had always promised its citizens.

Industrial capitalism, however, with its centralizing and monopolizing tendencies, challenged their traditional values of individualism, free competition, and equal opportunity, and was transforming America into a society of "haves and have-nots." They resisted this development, Montgomery argues. Indeed, Montgomery's important contribution to the discussion was the insight that the resulting class conflict, in which workers attempted to make the new and alien social order more humane and egalitarian, was a primary reason for the collapse of Radical Reconstruction. Northern labor leaders argued that, just as the South

---

[16] David Montgomery, *Beyond Equality: Labor and the Radical Republicans, 1862-1872,* Random House: New York, 1967.

was being reconstructed to create a more egalitarian society, so must the North also be reconstructed in the same way. The increasing class conflict in the North encouraged the captains of industry and Republican politicians to entertain second thoughts about the wisdom of an egalitarian southern Reconstruction.

Recent scholars have echoed Montgomery's interpretation of the Reconstruction Era. For example, in her 2001 book, *The Death of Reconstruction,* Heather Cox Richardson closely investigates postbellum newspapers, magazines, letters and speeches to persuasively argue that it was Northern class conflict, with its incessant challenges to the new industrial economy and calls for wealth redistribution, more than the virulent racism of the time, that contributed the most to the "death of Reconstruction."[17]

And, in fact, things were changing quickly in the wake of the Civil War. At the end of the Civil War in 1865, half or more of all adult Americans were self-employed and economically independent, but by 1870, according to that year's census, 70% of Americans were already directly or indirectly dependent upon wages, economically dependent, in other words, upon someone else.

Thus, to many observers it seemed that American civilization was on the brink of chaos and destruction, as the old order died and the newly emerging industrial capitalist order seemed inimical to the "American Promise" of equality. Within a short span of time they saw the United States transformed

[17]Heather Cox Richardson, *The Death of Reconstruction: Race, Labor, and Politics in the Post-Civil War North, 1865-1901,* Harvard University Press: Cambridge, 2001.

from an overwhelmingly agricultural society dominated by farmers, merchants, and small town artisans into an urban industrial society dominated by large factories, powerful corporations, and business elites. The changes challenged their ideas about the type of society America should be.

Herbert Gutman quotes Pittsburgh steel magnate Andrew Carnegie as boasting in his 1886 book, *Triumphant Democracy,* that, "The old nations of the earth creep on at a snail's pace, but the Republic thunders past with the rush of an express." But, Gutman goes on to say, "The articulate steelmaster...had missed the point. The very rapidity of the economic changes occurring in Carnegie's lifetime meant that many, unlike him, lacked the time, historically, culturally, and psychologically, to be separated or alienated from settled ways of work and life and from relatively fixed beliefs."[18]

Thus, Gutman says, "Certain elements in the preindustrial American social structure and in older patterns of popular ideology persisted strongly into the post-Civil War urban world, profoundly affected behavior, and served as a source of recurrent opposition to the power and status of the new industrialist."[19]

Basic to the ideas workers continued to hold into the postbellum years was, of course, the essentially middle class republican ideal of a good

---

[18]Herbert Gutman, *Work, Culture, and Society in Industrializing America: Essays in American Working-Class and Social History,* Vintage Books: New York, 1977, p. 272.

[19]Gutman, *Work, Culture, and Society in Industrializing America*, p. 29.

society. Gutman cites a coal miner speaking in 1876 who declared that, "The theory of Republicanism does not allow the laboring population to be reduced to poverty and dependence on the will of a few, and the virtual abrogation of our political rights and privileges."[20]

Historian Melvyn Dubofsky also notes that, "Both workers and industrialists might subscribe to the importance of home ownership. But what is one to make of Carnegie's multimillion-dollar Fifth Avenue mansion compared to the two-room shack of a coal miner? Workers, as well as employers, might boast about America's democratic-republican heritage, its Exceptionalism as a real 'people's republic.' But did democratic-republicanism carry precisely the same implications for both social classes? Certainly it seems likely that workers and industrialists might draw different meanings about the realities of the American political order from the facts of industrial conflict."[21]

And, indeed, the industrial conflict of the non-union era before the New Deal of the 1930s cannot be really understood without understanding these rival interpretations of what America was about.

Even so, these rival interpretations, existing even today, nevertheless were interpretations of the same widely held belief among Americans that "all men are created equal." The reason that belief was, and is, so widely held, however, is not because all

---

[20]Gutman, *Work, Culture, and Society in Industrializing America*, p. 29.

[21]Melvyn Dubofsky, *Industrialism and the American Worker, 1865-1920,* AHM Publishing Corp.: Arlington Heights, Illinois, 1975, p. 48.

Americans drank deeply from the well of Enlightenment rationalism. There was also another, more emotional, more plebian, stream that fed into the emerging American polity. That stream was the peculiar and exceptional variant of Christian theology that bloomed in early America and that had deep roots in the distant past.

While Lockian liberal republicanism may have bequeathed a secular language to describe the emerging American polity, there remained what Gutman termed, "older patterns of popular ideology." These older patterns of popular ideology emerged from a religious stream that ensured that Americans would deeply and widely adhere to the belief in fundamental equality for all Americans.

Ye Are All One in Christ Jesus

When the young French aristocrat Alexis de Tocqueville toured America in 1831-32, not long after the country became an independent nation, he was struck by the widespread material equality, at least among white male Americans. This is perhaps the most cited observation gleaned from his famous work, *Democracy in America*, published in two volumes in 1835 and 1840 and totaling more than 800 pages. "The more I advanced in the study of American society," he said, "the more I perceived that...equality of condition is the fundamental fact from which all others seem to be derived and the central point at which all my observations terminated."

But it was not just material conditions that de Tocqueville thought characterized American democracy. It was also the egalitarian "habits of the heart" of Americans, of which religious belief was foremost. French Enlightenment thinkers were critical of the Catholic Church and hostile to religion, hostility manifested prominently in the French Revolution. Indeed, these Enlightenment thinkers felt that democracy and religion were fundamentally incompatible.

But, in America, de Tocqueville found that religion was not only compatible with democracy, he felt it was absolutely fundamental to American democracy. Although there was no established church in America, nevertheless, he said, religion "must be considered as the first of America's institutions." It was religious belief, he felt, a widespread "habit of the heart," that explained American commitment to "equality of condition," and led them to value, for instance, universal and pragmatic general education for all over the esoteric education of elites.

More recent commentators on the origins of American democracy have taken issue with de Tocqueville's first-hand observations. Looking back after the closing of the frontier at the end of the nineteenth century, Frederick Jackson Turner famously declared that American democracy was *sui generis*, a utilitarian response of the pioneers to the endless and retreating frontier. For Turner, as Perry Miller phrased it, "democracy came out of the forest."[22]

Alternatively, commenting on the efforts of English parliamentarians in the sixteenth century to engross popular rights and political liberty, Edmund S. Morgan said, "Modern freedom may be considered in large measure an English invention, and some of the principal inventors were scholars who scoured the past for precedents to magnify the power of the House of Commons."[23]

Don Higginbotham acknowledges that the ideology of democracy may have been extant earlier, but the Revolution gave it life. "Such American ideas as sovereignty of the people, bills of rights, written

---

[22]Perry Miller, "Errand Into the Wilderness," in *Errand Into the Wilderness,* Harvard University Press: Cambridge, 1956, p. 1.

[23]Edmund S. Morgan, *American Slavery, American Freedom: The Ordeal of Colonial Virginia*, W. W. Norton & Co.: NY, 1975, p. 15.

constitutions, and separation of powers were all notions associated with the European Enlightenment, the so-called Age of Reason. It was the American Revolution, however, that transformed theories into political realities..."[24]

Other historians, beginning with Robert E. Brown in the 1950s, asserted flatly that *de facto* American political democracy existed prior to the Revolution. He argued that suffrage among property-owning church members was sufficiently broad-based in eighteenth century Massachusetts to warrant the designation of universal suffrage, thus creating a "middle-class democracy."[25]

In any case, whether uncovering the origins of American democracy in the Revolution, or earlier, in Europe or in the American forest, historians have for the most part been fairly uniform in situating the sources of American democracy firmly within the secular political tradition. Few have followed up on the point Brown raised only in passing. This was that the Congregational churches of the Puritans contained many democratic features, which surely must have informed the actions and attitudes of the populace, as 98% of all Massachusetts inhabitants were Congregationalists.[26]

---

[24] Don Higginbotham, *War and Society in Revolutionary America: The Wider Dimensions of Conflict*, University of South Carolina Press: Columbia, SC, 1988, p. 4.

[25] Robert E. Brown, *Middle-Class Democracy and the Revolution in Massachusetts, 1691-1780*, Russell & Russell: NY, 1955.

[26] Brown, p. 403. Even if Brown's figure of 98% is far too high, as other studies have suggested, this does not dilute the point of his argument.

Therefore, Brown argued, historians could not afford to ignore "religious democracy" as an additional influence on the Revolution and the kind of society that emerged from it. "We must remember," he said, "that the people of Massachusetts were accustomed to a church organization which lived by democratic procedures and opposition to the Church of England.... As many of them often said, religious and political freedoms were inextricably connected and would rise or fall together. Little wonder, then, that the Congregational clergy supported the Revolution almost to a man."[27]

Alexis de Tocqueville also noted this "religious democracy," this "first of America's institutions." It was something that he thought made American democracy so different from the concept of democracy held by European Enlightenment thinkers. However, he did not attempt to explicate its origin. Perhaps he was unable to do so. Indeed, to understand its origin, we must delve deeply into the history of Christianity, early America's dominant religion, back to the very origins of Christianity itself.

Once we do so, we discover much more than the hierarchical and authoritarian traditions in the religion to which European Enlightenment thinkers so strenuously objected. We also discover a powerful parallel tradition of equality and hostility to hierarchy and authority much older than the Enlightenment. Further, it was a parallel egalitarian tradition that could never be eradicated from the religion, because it was the belief and practice of the religion's very founders.

---

[27]Brown, p. 408.

The early primitive Christian church was one that proclaimed the complete equality of all believers in which, said St. Paul, "There is neither Greek nor Jew, circumcision nor uncircumcision, Barbarian, Scythian, bond nor free; but Christ is all, and in all" (Colossians 3:11). And, again, "There is neither Jew nor Greek, there is neither bond nor free, there is neither male nor female; for ye are all one in Christ Jesus" (Galatians 3:28). Indeed, said Paul in Athens, God "hath made of one blood all nations of men for to dwell on all the face of the earth" (Acts 17:26). This being the case, the Apostles even shared all material possessions in common, a form of primitive communism.

In a sense, one might thus term early Christianity a kind of "liberation theology." The early Christians took inspiration from the fact that Jesus was a lowly carpenter, a man of the people, who denied to Pontius Pilate that he was "the king of the Jews," as he was accused of thinking. Early Christianity was an oppositional movement that refused to worship the Roman emperor as divine, as did the Jews, and all the first Christians were, of course, Jews. It was an oppositional movement whose founder was murdered, crucified, by the empire, a form of punishment the empire reserved for political rebels.

In time, however, over the course of centuries, as this oppositional movement gained more followers and more power, things changed. Eventually, the church *against* Rome became the Church *of* Rome. It is commonly stated that the Emperor Constantine converted to Christianity. It would be more appropriate to say that Constantine converted Christianity to the needs of the empire, making it the official state religion. Paganism was suppressed, and all were required to become Christians. In this transformation, the foundational tradition of equality became overshadowed by the reality of power and hierarchy, of pomp and wealth. In the English Puritan formulation, this event marked the conquest of the Church by the Antichrist. John Milton, for instance, quoted Dante to declare that "the Romish Antichrist" (the Pope) was "merely bred up by Constantine."[28]

But, as Christianity became the established religion of the Roman Empire, and a self-justifying theology of authority and hierarchy developed, the original egalitarian tradition could never be entirely disowned. It was always there to be drawn upon as a constant source of tension within the Church. This was because it was embedded in the very foundational teachings of the religion and had the unassailable authority of apostolic endorsement.[29]

---

[28]See Christopher Hill, *Antichrist in Seventeenth-Century England*, Oxford University Press: London, 1971, p. 94.

[29]Note that the rallying cry of the Jewish Zealots, contemporaries of Jesus, in their war against Rome was, "No King but God!" Jewish liturgy yet retains this phrase as, "We have no king besides you." Richard Landes says this "...may be taken as the motto of egalitarian monotheism: God's rule over all men precludes the rule of man over man." See his "Literacy and the Origins of Inquisitorial Christianity: The Exegetical Battle Between Hierarchy and Community in the Christian Empire (300-500 CE," unpublished paper, University of Pittsburgh, 1989, p. 12. For an example of the classic anti-monarchical tradition in Judaism, see the prophet Samuel's warnings against kings in I Samuel, 8:7-8.

This foundational culture of opposition, constantly referred back to, contained vivid imagery that provided the oppressed of all eras a continuing ideology of opposition and a vocabulary to express their yearnings for freedom. As E. P. Thompson points out, it is through this imagery of "Babylon and the Egyptian exile and the Celestial City and the contest with Satan [that] minority groups have articulated their experience and projected their aspirations for hundreds of years… It is a sign of how men felt and hoped, loved and hated, and of how they preserved certain values in the very texture of their language."[30]

It was this egalitarian, anti-authoritarian tradition that engendered the continually recurring schisms and heresies that plagued the Church. By referring back to first principals, the true believers saw orthodoxy (being hierarchical) as a betrayal of the true faith. Despite the best efforts of the authorities, heresies based upon this egalitarian culture, such as the Waldensians, could not be permanently eradicated without destroying the religion itself. Thus, they periodically reappeared in heretical, oppositional movements that used the very

---

Cromwell's Puritan army resurrected a reformulation of this phrase, "No king but Jesus," during the English Civil War. Christopher Hill terms this concept a "built-in anarchy" because "The doctrine that Christ alone rules over the elect…is ultimately a doctrine of anarchy: the individual (or the congregation) is subordinate to no earthly authority, but only to the Holy Spirit within." See Christopher Hill, *Antichrist in Seventeenth-Century England*, p. 169.

[30] E. P. Thompson, *The Making of the English Working Class*, Vintage Books: NY, 1963, p. 49.

language and traditions of the Church against the Church.

Given the religious nature of the culture, it was inevitable that social protest and rebellion would also be seen and expressed in religious terms. We find this phenomenon even before the Reformation of the 1500s. According to the chronicler Thomas Walsingham, during the English Peasants' Revolt of 1381, the renegade priest John Ball delivered a sermon to the assembled peasants voicing their opposition to serfdom with the famous words, "When Adam delved and Eve span, who was then a gentleman?" This was a formulation that may have even dated back several centuries before 1381.

This religious egalitarian ethos is also found in the enduring English "Piers Plowman" tradition of socio-religious protest. William Langland, for example, writing in the 1300s, elevated the lowly and wrapped his protest in the mantle of apostolic authority. He attacked privilege and wealth, both secular and clerical, saying,

> God is often in the gorge of these great masters,
> But among the lowly men are his mercy and his works…
> Clerics and other conditions converse of God readily,
> And have him much in the mouth,
> But mean men in their hearts…
> Our Prince Jesus and His Apostles chose poverty together,
> And the longer they lived, the less wealth they mastered.[31]

---

[31]William Langland, "The Vision of Piers Plowman," in James Bruce Ross & Mary Martin McLaughlin, *The*

But Langland was not merely praising the ancient lowly and communal poverty. Contained within the Piers Plowman protest tradition was also the belief in the natural equality of the highest and lowest, for God "Sends forth the sun to shine on the villein's [peasant's] tillage as brightly as on the best man's and on the best woman's."[32]

Similar sentiments were expressed by German peasants during the bloody Peasants' Revolt of 1524-25, when the lowly farmers across the southern and central Holy Roman Empire rose up against their princely overlords in Europe's largest peasant revolt. That revolt produced a flurry of radical pamphlets justifying their revolt in religious terms. One of the most important, "The Twelve Articles of the Peasantry," called for the abolition of serfdom, and did so for religious reasons. "It has been customary until now," it said, "to hold us as bonds people, which is to be deplored, as Christ redeemed and purchased us all with the precious shedding of his blood, the shepherd as much as the highest noble."

The Peasants' Revolt was a class war, but the peasants justified their demands for secular and physical liberation in terms of the universally recognized spiritual redemption from bondage obtained from the sacrifice of Jesus upon the cross. Friedrich Engels, much more interested in religion than his colleague Karl Marx, recognized this in his *The Peasant War in Germany*. In that work he discussed how the revolutionary aspirations of the

---

Portable Medieval Reader, The Viking Press: NY, 1949, pp. 196, 198.

[32]Langland, p. 199.

peasantry took a religious form, and the secular political significance of such spiritual beliefs.

The Protestant Reformation, sparked by renegade Catholic priest Martin Luther's condemnations of the departure of the Catholic Church from the foundational teachings of the apostles, was also a revolution engendered by an appeal to the first principles of the religion itself. In turn, its success was an instigation to yet further challenges to religious authority. Thus, the period from 1500 to 1650 encompassed not only the Reformation but also numerous large and widespread wars and peasant revolts. All of them found inspiration in a "return to basics," a time when society was more just, more equitable, enlivened by a more "pure" form of Christianity. Indeed, says Helen White, speaking of social protest in England at this time, "This was the great age of the appeal to the example of the primitive church."[33]

And there was much protest at this time in England, as it was the time of the enclosures of public farmlands and grazing lands by the great landlords. This economic protest, however, was often framed in religious terms, so much so that it became difficult to separate the threads of motivation. In the late 1540s a spate of rebellions flickered across the English countryside in places such as Devon, Norfolk, Exeter and Cornwall. As White notes, "Certainly religious unrest had the major role in the rebellions of Exeter and Cornwall...[and] there had been some traces of

[33]Helen C. White, *Social Criticism in Popular Religious Literature of the Sixteenth Century*, The Macmillan Co.: NY, 1944, p. 111.

social unrest in the religious demands of the western rebels of 1549."[34]

These English uprisings often demanded a type of egalitarian society reminiscent of the primitive Church. Describing the rebels of 1548, one of the King's Commissioners said, "Some be Anabaptists and libertines, and would have all things [in] common." This description was echoed in 1550 by Thomas Lever, who said the anti-enclosure rebels believed that, "there should be no rich men or rulers."[35] Instead, said one minister in 1549, these rebels believed that, "The poorest ploughman is in Christ equal with the greatest prince that is."[36]

Half a century later, in the Midland Revolt of 1607, both enclosures and revolts against them continued, with the rebels expressing the same sentiments. Religiously inspired rebels rose in numerous locales, such as Derbyshire, Bedfordshire, Lincolnshire, Leicestershire, and Staffordshire. In discussing these insurgencies, Roger B. Manning emphasized that they were not motivated simply by economics, but also had definite religious overtones. "One should avoid the temptation," he said, "to view the Midland Revolt of 1607 merely as a series of enclosure riots...like the rebellions of 1549 the Midland Revolt also was distinguished by...behavior usually characteristic of adherents of millenarian movements."[37]

---

[34] White, p. 116.

[35] White, pp. 121, 118.

[36] White, p. 123.

[37] Roger B. Manning, *Village Revolts: Social Protest and Popular Disturbances in England, 1509-1640*, Clarendon Press: Oxford, 1988, p. 235.

Helen White suggests that the enduring inspiration, the intellectual resource, for these popular revolts by commoners was a religious reference back to first principles. For instance, she cites a satirical play of the 1590s lampooning "Parson Ball," the renegade Catholic priest John Ball, who was a spokesman for the rebellious peasants of 1381, two hundred years before! Evidently discerning the same religious motivations between the peasant rebels of the two widely separated ages, despite the passage of centuries, the play has Parson Ball preaching that,

> England is grown to such a pass of late,
> That rich men triumph to see the poor beg at their gate.
> But I am able by good scripture before you to prove,
> That God doth not this dealing allow nor love,
> But when Adam delved, and Eve span,
> Who was then a Gentleman?
> Brethren, it were better to have this Community,
> Than to have this difference in degrees.[38]

Mock this belief as they may, the religious authorities could not deny the source of the communal agitation: Their own apostolic traditions and foundational teachings.

The religious nature of the Thirty Years' War (1618-1648) intensified these egalitarian and even millennial tendencics inherent in Christianity, as it convinced many that the bloody conflict between Catholic and Protestant forces was, in fact, a precursor to the final conflict of Armageddon. The Last Days were at hand as good Protestant Christians battled the Roman Antichrist and Jesus would soon

[38] White, p. 120.

come in His glory to usher in the Kingdom of Heaven. John Milton spoke of Christ as the "shortly-expected king" and John Bunyan declared that, "the judgement day is at hand."[39]

These religiously inspired rumblings, centuries old in England, finally found a political expression in the English Civil War of the 1640s. The extremely egalitarian Diggers, for example, explicitly believed the civil war meant that the Second Coming of Christ was at hand and that "Jesus Christ...will dwell in the whole creation, that is, in every man and woman without exception," bringing with him the ultimate democratization of salvation.[40]

Therefore, argued Michael Mullett, speaking specifically of the Quakers, Levelers, and Diggers in England, it is impossible to understand the radical egalitarian movements of the Puritan Revolution if one ignores this religious inspiration because "The Diggers used history, Scripture history, to back up their case."[41] Indeed, declared Gerrard Winstanley, the leader of the Diggers, "Jesus Christ...is the head Leveller."[42]

But, it was not just the more extreme Puritans, such as the Levelers and Diggers, who expressed such sentiments. The feeling was widespread, as "Puritans perceived...a critical role

---

[39] Christopher Hill, *The World Turned Upside Down: Radical Ideas During the English Revolution*, Penguin Books: Harmondworth, UK, 1975, pp. 96, 97.

[40] Michael Mullett, *Radical Religious Movements in Early Modern Europe*, George Allen & Unwin: London, 1980, p. 54.

[41] Mullett, p. 53.

[42] Christopher Hill, *Antichrist*, p. 117.

for themselves in defending the gospel. To them the cosmic struggles of the Apocalypse were not so much a matter of study as of participation.... In such militancy lay the psychological roots of the famous apocalyptic morale of Oliver Cromwell's troopers."[43]

The Errand into the Wilderness

However, even before the Puritan Revolution in England, some true believers felt that the Church of England was so polluted and permeated with the Mark of the Beast, the Antichrist, that it was impossible to "purify" it. "The separatists say we are in the midst of Babylon," declared a Churchman in 1624.[44] Indeed, the Church of England was a kind of Babylonian Captivity to them, for the Antichrist had "...forced the unregenerate into the church alongside the godly. The elect must separate themselves both from the antichristian ministry and from the ungodly multitude who are compelled to participate in Anglican worship. A voluntary gathering of the saints is opposed to the state-compulsive assemblies of Antichrist."[45]

Therefore, and especially since the Second Coming was nigh, it was incumbent upon all good Christians to separate themselves from the Church's corruption, which many Puritans, including those who landed at Plymouth in 1620, proceeded to do. And, as they left for New England, they took their

---

[43] J. F. Maclear, "New England and the Fifth Monarchy: The Quest for the Millennium in Early American Puritanism," *The William and Mary Quarterly*, V. 32, No. 2, April, 1975, p. 226.

[44] Hill, *Antichrist*, p. 53.

[45] Hill, *Antichrist*, p. 60.

religious beliefs and practices with them, forming an even more extremely "purified" variant of Puritanism in New England than the variant left behind in Old England.

Between 1630 and 1641 nearly 16,000 of the faithful separated themselves from "Babylon", as many had come to term Old England. Most did so because they expected its imminent destruction. "Few themes are more prevalent in migration literature," says J. F. Maclear, "than that of Old England's impending 'desolation,' a dread sentence that moved orthodox and heterodox alike, Richard Mather and Hooker as well as Anne Hutchinson, to seek overseas refuge." Indeed, shocked by the primitive condition of frontier Boston upon her arrival, Anne Hutchinson exclaimed, "If she had not a sure word that England should be destroyed, her heart would shake."[46] There, claimed Perry Miller, these most pure of the Puritans would build "a city on a hill" that would be a beacon of righteousness to the world, an example of how saints everywhere would shortly live together in peace and saintly equality after the advent of Christ.

Necessarily, this removal to New England meant more than a new religious settlement of true saints gathered together into a purified and egalitarian congregation of the faithful. It also meant a new form of purified and more egalitarian civil government built upon that church model. Ultimately, one implied the other, for, as E. P. Thompson pointed out, "Their attachment to civil and religious liberty went hand in hand."[47]

---

[46]Maclear, pp. 230, 240.
[47]Thompson, p. 53.

Thus, in the New World, these Puritans clearly expected to establish a new civil polity, along with a new church. For instance, argues David B. Quinn, the Rev. William Crashaw preached a sermon in 1609 before Lord La Warre, Governor of Virginia, in which "he stressed the opportunity offered to planters in Virginia to become 'Fathers and Founders of a new Church and Commonwealth.'"

Thus, "If by moving from London to Jamestown, settlers really acquired the right to add something 'new' to the Church, then by flying from London to Amsterdam or Leyden a 'gathered church' might claim the right to inject something 'new' into its polity, either in the Netherlands or in America, if it should move there."[48]

The fact that the early Puritan settlers of New England came, not for economic gain, but primarily for religious purposes is evident again and again in the testimonies of those early inhabitants. For example, Edward Winslow, one early Plymouth inhabitant plainly stated why he and his fellow saints came to the New World. "We came here to avoid the hierarchy, the holy days, the Book of Common Prayer, etc."[49] For one attuned to the nuances of the Puritan idiom, it would be clear that "hierarchy" was a code word referring to the governing structure of the Church of England. Other code words commonly appearing in their speech included, "popery," "Antichrist," and "Babylon." For instance, historian

---

[48]David B. Quinn, "The First Pilgrims," *The William and Mary Quarterly*, V. XXIII, No. 3, July, 1966, p. 363.
[49]Quoted in Sumner Chilton Powell, *Puritan Village: The Formation of a New England Town*, Wesleyan University Press: Middletown, CT, 1963, p. xviii.

Paul Christianson points out that, "English reformers...normally reserved the term 'antichrist' for the leading human instrument of evil on earth [the Pope], 'Babylon' for the institutional form of his power."[50] Within this framework, "hierarchy" quite specifically referred to the authoritarian, antichristian, governmental structure in the Church of England. This is made clear, for instance, in the title of a 1641 Puritan treatise, "Reasons Why The Hierarchy, or Government of the Church."[51]

Such sentiments were not confined entirely to the Puritans who landed and settled in Massachusetts. As they spread out into the New England hinterland, they carried their worldviews with them. Thus, for instance the founders of Portsmouth, Rhode Island sought to govern themselves by the Mosaic laws they deduced from biblical precedent. Before leaving Boston they pledged themselves in a covenant declaring, "We, whose names are underwritten, do here solemnly, in the presence of Jehovah, incorporate ourselves into a Body Politic and, as He shall help, will submit our persons, lives, and estates unto our Lord, Jesus Christ, the King of Kings and Lord of Lords, and to all those perfect and most absolute laws of His given us in his holy word of truth, to be guided and judged thereby."[52]

What might this new saintly polity look like? Already by 1580 Puritan Separatists in England had

---

[50]Paul Christianson, *Reformers and Babylon: English Apocalyptic Visions from the Reformation to the Eve of the Civil War*, University of Toronto Press: Toronto, Canada, 1978, p. 9.

[51]Christianson, p. 263.

[52]Quoted in Maclear, p. 241.

emerged under Queen Elizabeth and were already viewed as seeking "concepts of a Utopian society."[53] A critic of the Separatists in 1616 highlighted this search for a new political order when he claimed they were seeking "Sir Thomas Moore's Utopia, or rather Plato's Community..." Commenting on this remark, David B. Quinn states that the use of these terms to describe the political goals of Separatism, "namely Plato's *Republic* and More's *Utopia*," clearly indicated a recognition of "...their separation from the established order in politics, no less than in religion."[54]

The Puritan Separatists who landed at Plymouth in 1620, being all saints and all, therefore, equal, expected to await Christ's imminent arrival by living together peacefully in a pure communion of the godly. John Locke, in his *Second Treatise on Civil Government*, pointed to their Mayflower Compact of 1620, written aboard their ship before landing, as an example of a secular social contract establishing a civil form of government agreed to by free and equal property owners. It was thus, claimed Locke, a sign of their secular Enlightenment commitment to civil liberty. Most commentators echo Locke in this regard when they discuss the Mayflower Compact.

But, contrary to Locke, that Compact, signed by all the equal Puritan saints on board the Mayflower, claimed that they were engaged in an endeavor, "Undertaken for the Glory of God and Advancement of the Christian Faith." It was, Henry

---

[53] Quinn, p. 363.
[54] Quinn, p. 387.

Steele Commager pointed out, "an extension of the customary church covenant to civil circumstances."[55]

It seems clear, then, that many New England Puritans made a conscious and deliberate effort to hew closely to their Scriptural guide in establishing the civil governments of their little commonwealths. In this way, New England townsmen acquired the habit and expectation of self-government, within the context of their Puritan theology and practice. People, then, took with them into town politics the tradition of democracy taught them by their faith. This, in turn, made possible the triumph of the famous egalitarian New England town meeting.

The errand into the wilderness, however, was not just a democratic compact between equal saints. It was also a covenant with God. John Wintrop, who was to become Governor of the Massachusetts Bay Colony in Boston, emphasized this in his 1629 sermon, "A Model of Christian Charity," preached aboard the Arbella in mid-Atlantic en route to Massachusetts Bay. "We have drawn up indentures with the Almighty," Perry Miller paraphrased him as saying. Part of that agreement with the Almighty was to form a "due form of Government, both civil and ecclesiastical" in Massachusetts. As Miller points out, "There was no doubt whatsoever about what Winthrop meant by a due form of ecclesiastical government. He meant the pure biblical polity set forth in full detail by the New Testament."[56] This, of course, was a polity based upon apostolic democracy in rejection of the Antichrist's hierarchical strictures.

---

[55]Henry Steele Commager, *Documents in American History*, Appleton-Century-Crofts: NY, 1963, p. 15.
[56]Perry Miller, "Errand Into the Wilderness," p. 5.

Other scholars have found corroborating evidence for Miller's contention. Thus, Theodore Dwight Bozeman says that, "In the great majority of cases, religiously activated migrants described their departure from England...as a search for 'liberty of the ordinances'; often this was joined to a venomous critique both of 'ceremonies' and of 'human inventions' in the Church of England."[57]

The dominant feature of the New England Puritan covenant with God, Bozeman says, was the promise to establish a pure Church, one based upon the primitive apostolic church. "Progress in Christian reform," he states, "was simultaneously a retrogression, for the very means of advance into greater purity and towards eschatological vindication was retrieval of the ancient and unspoilt. Thus as dissenting voices portrayed the moral and ecclesiastical changes that alone would ensure the national welfare, they called men back to contemplate...ancient Israel; so, too, in their particular fever against the 'rags of popery' in the present church, they practically made a career of appealing to 'the Apostles' time, when all things were pure...'"[58]

This appeal to apostolic precedent in the Puritan search for the authentic roots of their relationship to God always resulted in a greater emphasis on equality and democracy in church and state. For instance, Bozeman examined many New

[57]Theodore Dwight Bozeman, "Biblical Primitivism: An Approach to New England Puritanism," in Richard T. Hughes, Editor, *The American Quest for the Primitive Church*, University of Illinois Press: Urbana, 1988, p. 25.
[58]Bozeman, pp. 23, 26.

England governmental documents, most notably the Cambridge Platform of 1648. In every case he found that they exhibited a widely democratic emphasis in their search for a more apostolic inspiration. "Thus," he said, "the proposition that 'the church of the brethren was the power...to choose their officers' was grounded upon the use of 'vote and suffrage' in the selection of Judas's successor in the apostolic band (Acts 1:15); upon the election of elders in the earliest church in Antioch 'by lifting up of hands' (Acts 14:23); or upon the Apostles' instructions to the saints gathered in Jerusalem to elect a staff of seven deacons; and similar instances (Acts 6:3, 5, 7)."[59]

Philip F. Gura also found an egalitarian democratic zeal, based upon an appeal to first principles, as basic to what he termed, "The central dynamic at the core of Puritan ideology."[60] Further, it was the struggle between more radical Puritans seeking even more democracy and the traditional Congregationalists, he claims, that shaped the "New England Way" and formed American political ideology. What we now identify as New England Congregationalism, he said, evolved out of "A sharp and continual debate with those who from their English Puritan experience had formed a particularly democratic notion of their errand into America's wilderness."[61]

Even more specifically, Gura went on to declare, "I believe that the ecclesiastical and doctrinal

---

[59]Bozeman, p. 28.

[60]Philip F. Gura, *A Glimpse of Sion's Glory: Puritan Radicalism in New England, 1620-1660*, Wesleyan University Press: Middletown, CT, 1984, p. 305.

[61]Gura, p. 11.

underpinnings of New England theology evolved as a result of a constant dialectic between non-separating Congregationalists and those in the population who argued for more radical reorganization of seventeenth century society...in many ways our national ideology was formed by a co-optation of a more radical agenda for our political and social priorities."[62]

In New England, Congregational leaders such as John Winthrop, who had been dissidents in Old England, became the new authorities. As such, they attempted to stop the flow of history and claimed that they had at last arrived at the perfect form of pure and godly government, both spiritual and secular.

But others in their midst viewed the new authorities as simply a new hierarchy and, by appealing to the same model of the primitive church, rejected what they saw as the authoritarianism of the New England Jerusalem. Such criticism of the new authorities emerged even in Puritan Plymouth, as Gura discovered. "As private and peaceful as Plymouth was, it...held within its borders volatile elements, for the separatists' aspirations toward a purity of worship comparable to that enjoyed in the apostolic churches did, in fact, encourage restless souls to question the purity of *any* ordinances in this, a fallen world, and, in some cases, the very necessity of organized worship itself."[63]

All of this internal tumult, of course, was in the search for the most authentic, the most "pure" religion that would demonstrate to the brethren still back in the Babylon of Old England how to prepare, politically, as well as spiritually, for the imminent

---

[62]Gura, p. viii.
[63]Gura, p. 32.

coming of the Lord. "These Puritans did not flee to America," Miller said. "They went in order to work out that complete reformation which was not yet accomplished in England and Europe, but which would quickly be accomplished if only the saints back there had a working model to guide them.... This errand was being run for the sake of Reformed Christianity; and while the first aim was indeed to realize in America the due form of government, both civil and ecclesiastical, the aim behind that aim was to vindicate the most rigorous ideal of the Reformation, so that ultimately all Europe would imitate New England"[64]

This ultimate expectation of the New England saints can be seen in much of John Cotton's Boston sermons, preached most particularly in his 1641, "The Church's Resurrection." In it he claimed that New England's "fair preparation" for the coming millennium led the world toward the light, and the time would soon come when, "Those that were branded before for Huguenots, and Lollards, and Heretics, they shall be thought the only men fit to have crowns upon their heads and independent government committed to them for a thousand years together."[65]

And, claims Miller, Winthrop and his fellow saints made "wonderfully good" in their effort to establish a pure and godly polity in New England. Unfortunately for them, in the meantime the saints who remained behind in Babylon set about constructing their own model of the ideal polity under Cromwell's Commonwealth. This made the errand

---

[64]Miller, "Errand Into the Wilderness," pp. 11, 12.
[65]Quoted in Maclear, p. 234.

into the wilderness moot. "If an actor," said Miller, "playing the leading role in the greatest dramatic spectacle of the century, were to attire himself and put on his makeup, rehearse his lines, take a deep breath, and stride onto the stage, only to find the theater dark and empty, no spotlight working, and himself entirely alone, he would feel as did New England around 1650 or 1660. For in the 1640s, during the Civil Wars, the colonies, so to speak, lost their audience."[66]

Thus, the "errand" of establishing a precedent-setting model of authentic government was irrelevant during the period of the Commonwealth, for New Jerusalem was actually being constructed by the "Bare Bones" Parliament, a parliament of saints, back in Old England. After the Restoration of the monarchy in 1660, the errand became even more irrelevant, indeed, something under the monarchy to be repudiated.

But, Gura insisted that appearances could be deceiving. Given the "centrifugal dynamic" of Puritanism, any triumph of authority is only temporary, and therefore, "Try as they might, the New England theocrats were powerless to control the antiauthoritarian, democratic, impulse at the heart of the Puritan revolution...the revolution of the saints could not be restricted.... because it already had occurred implicitly, in the magistrates' and ministers' incorporation of the notions of visible sainthood and corporate selfhood into the colony's public ideology, and thus in the creation of a state in which the individual, no matter who he was or what he did, possessed a dignity and purpose unavailable to him

---

[66]Miller, "Errand Into the Wilderness," p. 13.

elsewhere in the Protestant world...New England...in fact encouraged a true revolution of the saints."[67]

Thus, much of the radically egalitarian Puritan worldview was incorporated into the secular political ideology. For this reason, Gura argues, radical Puritanism should be seen not only as a precursor to the Great Awakening, but to the American Revolution itself. "In one form or another, Puritan radicalism was unquestionably an important influence in American theology until at least the time of the Great Awakening; whether it contributed significantly to the political ideology of the American Revolution is still very much open to consideration...[because] no one has yet detailed the connections between this radicalism, particularly the American patriots' powerful anti-authoritarianism and their millennial aspirations, and the tradition of seventeenth century American radicalism."[68]

The Great Awakening

If Puritan egalitarian radicalism was "unquestionably" a great influence on American theology up to the time of the Great Awakening, perhaps we should look at the nature of that religious revival that swept the American colonies from 1739-1742. There had been a brief effervescence of religious enthusiasm in Northampton, Massachusetts, in 1734-35, presided over by the Rev. Jonathan Edwards. But the beginning of the Great Awakening itself was sparked by the arrival in the colonies of British evangelist George Whitefield. He first attracted enthusiastic crowds in Georgia and

---

[67]Gura, pp. 14-15.
[68]Gura, pp. 326-327.

Charleston, South Carolina. Then he toured the entire Atlantic seaboard in 1739-40, with the revival following in his wake.

From the beginning, it was evident that the Awakening was not only a religious controversy, but a political one, as well. This was so because the revivalists were primarily itinerant ministers, like Whitefield, who preached the sanctity of individual religious experience and conscience in a society of settled ministers serving politically established churches. In the South, the Anglican Church (as the Church of England was called in America) was the official state church. Meanwhile, except for Rhode Island, the Congregationalist churches of New England had gradually accrued almost as much official power. It was therefore inevitable that a conflict between an "awakened" laity and a recalcitrant clergy for control of the direction of religious practice would also be a struggle between the people and the state for liberty of conscience. As Mark L. Sargent noted, "At once an appeal for biblical orthodoxy and a rebellion against church tradition, the Great Awakening posed its most severe threat to the social hierarchy of both church and state."[69]

Gilbert Tennent, a leader of the Awakening, highlighted the political aspects of this struggle in his pamphlet, *The Danger of an Unconverted Ministry*. Perry Miller and Alan Heimert term this "The manifesto of the revivalist party [and] the most influential sermon of the Awakening, and perhaps of

---

[69]Mark L. Sargent, "Plymouth Rock and the Great Awakening," *Journal of American Studies*, No. 22, 1988, p. 253.

the century."[70] In this pamphlet, Tennent championed itinerant preachers, such as himself, and said that it was proper for the laity to abandon their own ministers for "the greater good." Thus, "Tennent directly challenged the traditional parochial basis of church and society. From the resulting controversy…there emerged opposing conceptions of the church. The anti-revival party saw the church as a structured hierarchy, the power and weight of which was felt eventually in a particular community. The pro-revivalists, who defined the church as a means of spreading the gospel, emphasized the unalienable rights of the laity."[71]

The "woke" who had been "awakened" argued that only the laity, the common people of the church, rightly had the authority and legitimacy to govern the church. Where they could not convince their ministers of this view, they left their thus revealed "unconverted ministers" and the "standing order" in Massachusetts and Connecticut to establish "Separate," more egalitarian, congregations controlled by the laity.

They also placed an emphasis on what Jonathan Edwards called "experimental religion," meaning that religious grace was properly "experienced" in the "affections" or emotions, rather than through accepted church doctrine. Likewise, God's grace experienced by the untutored plain folk was of far greater value than all the teachings of the

---

[70]Perry Miller and Alan Heimert, Editors, *The Great Awakening: Documents Illustrating the Crisis and Its Consequences,* The Bobbs-Merrill Co., Inc.: NY, 1967, p. xxxiv.

[71]Miller and Heimert, p. xxxiv.

"Pharisee Teachers" at Harvard and Yale, both centers of ministerial opposition to the Awakening.

In addition to the hostility toward the elites, the authorities in the universities and the established clergy, those who were "Awakened" emphasized the essential equality of all the Awakened, regardless of their circumstances. One of the examples of how far this attitude was carried can be seen in what happened in Plymouth. Both George Whitefield and Gilbert Tennent went to Plymouth and, at the invitation of the laity, preached against the dangers of unconverted clergy from the pulpit of the First Church of Plymouth, the oldest church in New England. The Rev. Andrew Croswell, another itinerant "New Light" evangelist and believer in the Awakening, then brought the crisis in Plymouth to a climax. He preached against "settled Pastors" and "Pharisee Ministers" from the pulpit of the Plymouth church all day, from dawn to dusk, every day of the week, for two weeks. "Foremost among Croswell's sins, according to the Old Lights in Plymouth, was his effort to democratize the worship service by inviting women, children, and Negroes into the pulpit in complete disregard for the authority and training of the clergy."[72]

The result of this rebellion of the laity at the First Church of Plymouth was a schism. Since the "Awakened" laity had taken control of the church, Elder Thomas Faunce led the conservatives in establishing a second congregation still loyal to "religious conformity and political conservatism

---

[72]Sargent, p. 253.

that...resisted pluralism and appeals for the wider distribution of power."[73]

Thus, the Great Awakening resulted in a war of ideas that shattered the old religious and political order that had evolved over time in the Colonies. Indeed, many historians view the Great Awakening as a direct precursor of the Revolution. Speaking specifically of Connecticut, for instance, Robert Sklar contends that, "The Great Awakening...was the single most significant event of eighteenth century Connecticut, almost more important to the Revolution than the war itself, for the religious revival became a struggle to throw off the tyranny of old ideas. Almost every colony before the War of Independence went through an experience, which demonstrated, to paraphrase John Adams, that the Revolution was first won in the minds of the people.... The Great Awakening changed the direction of political and social development in Connecticut colony, pointing it and thrusting it forward toward revolution and independence."[74]

Perry Miller and Alan Heimert agree with Sklar's assessment, not just for Connecticut, but also for the American colonies as a whole. "What was wrought by the Great Awakening" they said, "was a profound alteration in ideas and aspirations.... Rapidly and radically Calvinism's vision of the social good flowed into political protest, into challenges to the 'rulers' of colonial society, and, eventually, into

---

[73]Sargent, p. 255.

[74]Robert Sklar, "The Great Awakening and Colonial Politics: Connecticut's Revolution in the Minds of Men," *Connecticut Historical Society*, V. 28, No. 3, July, 1963, p. 81.

the discussion and the activity that preceded and accompanied the American Revolution... in the Great Awakening the 'will of the people' began its steady march to eventual supremacy.... What was awakened in 1740 was the spirit of American democracy."[75]

Virginia on the Eve of the Revolution

The Great Awakening, of course, was not confined to Plymouth, Connecticut, or even New England. George Whitefield, for instance, had first begun his preaching in Georgia and South Carolina, working his way up the Atlantic seaboard. Thus, the Awakening swept all the Colonies, and Rhys Isaac agrees that it had a profound political impact in Virginia. There, "The Established Church was an integral part of the fabric of colonial Virginia society and its system of authority.... Fundamental shifts in values and organization that occur outside and against existing structures are highly subversive of established authority. The spread of concern for vital religion challenged the hegemony of the gentry..."[76]

Things soon became even worse for the local constituted authorities as the evangelical Awakened Baptists began proselytizing. "The confrontation between evangelicalism and the traditional order," Isaac tells us, "entered into its fiercest and most bitter phase as the New Light Separate Baptists moved into the longer-settled parts of Virginia in the years after 1765."[77] These Awakened "Could seek refuge in a

[75]Miller and Heimert, pp. lvi, lviii, lx-lxi.

[76]Rhys Isaac, *The Transformation of Virginia, 1740-1790,* University of North Carolina Press: Chapel Hill, NC, 1982, pp. 157, 265.

[77]Isaac, p. 162.

close, supportive, and orderly community, 'a congregation of faithful persons, called out of the world by divine grace, who mutually agree to live together, and execute gospel discipline among them.'"[78]

These Awakened Baptists also brought their dangerous egalitarian ideas with them and were, for instance, the only populations in Virginia and elsewhere in the South who challenged slavery before 1800. The Virginia Awakened Baptists just prior to the Revolution preached an elevation of the lowly, extending even to slaves, in contrast to the "corrupt" larger community. This commitment to equality among the community of Awakened saints, independent of external authority, was extremely threatening, especially in a slave society. Isaac notes that, "It was a particular mark of the Baptists' radicalism...that they included the slaves as 'brothers' and 'sisters' in their close communities.... The success of the Baptists among the slaves was spectacular and inspired a good deal of hostility of gentlemen in the legislature who sought to curb the expansion of the movement.... The Baptists' following may have amounted to as much as ten percent of the population by 1772. More alarming for those wedded to the traditional system was the movement's rate of growth. In 1769 only seven Separate Baptist churches were constituted in Virginia, with no more than three of them located in the longer-settled regions north of the James. By October, 1774, the number had climbed to fifty-four in all – twenty-four north of the James."[79]

---

[78] Isaac, pp. 164-165.
[79] Isaac, pp. 165, 171, 172.

It was inevitable, given the official status of the Anglican Church in Virginia as the established "state religion" that religious opposition to the Church became political opposition to constituted authorities. This was especially true since the power of the state was used to repress religious dissidents. This bred great bitterness among the Awakened Baptists and, as the movement reached its crest in 1771-1774, on the very eve of the Revolution, their antagonism to the church-state relationship took on the aura of ancient religious protests. Among the 4,000-5,000 delegates to the first convention of the Virginia Separate Baptists Association in 1771, Isaac tells us, "Defiance of authority was rife".[80]

By the end of 1771 at least 20 itinerant Baptist preachers had been arrested and jailed. This did not, however, stop them from proselytizing. "Often they preached through the bars from the prison to followers outside; and in one case the exasperated justices were reduced to building a wall around the jail to prevent such communication.... Facing repression from the civil authorities, some Baptists turned their denunciations in that direction also." This led some authorities to fear that Virginia was "verging fast towards republicanism and puritanism."[81]

Awakened Baptists began to challenge political institutions "formerly regarded as sacrosanct... [including] the efficacy of the county courts and the qualifications of the justices...the social status of jurors was deplored; graver misgivings than ever surrounded the college; and by

---

[80]Isaac, p. 192.
[81]Isaac, p. 172.

1774 even the structure of authority in the militia was called into question."[82]

The struggle between the traditional order and the Awakened Baptists continued for another ten years, right up to and through the Revolution, contributing in large measure to the revolutionary upheaval in Virginia. All of this calls into question the famous contention of Edmund S. Morgan that ideas of equality espoused by Virginians during this period were made possible by the very existence of slavery. Morgan presented us with a united white front of equals – who were considered to be "equal" because they weren't slaves.[83] Therefore, Virginians could be in the forefront of republican agitation against Britain at this time, as in their opposition to the 1765 Stamp Act, while remaining slave owners because their racism excluded slaves from consideration. "Racism," said Morgan, "made it possible for white Virginians to develop a devotion to the equality that English republicans had declared to be the soul of liberty."[84]

But Morgan never mentions the Great Awakening in his famous work, nor the Awakened Baptist movement at this time, a movement that rose up the humblest amongst them, including slaves, to equality. Indeed, the Awakened Baptists even sent out slaves to preach the gospel of equality to both whites and blacks! The Awakened Baptist shattering of the united white front to embrace even slaves as

---

[82]Isaac, p. 199.

[83]Edmund S. Morgan, *American Slavery, American Freedom: The Ordeal of Colonial Virginia*, W. W. Norton & Co.: NY, 1975, p. 381.

[84]Morgan, p. 386.

"brothers and sisters" in their congregations casts serious doubt on Morgan's assertion that American slavery of blacks made possible American freedom for whites.

Further, according to Isaac, the Awakened Baptist movement, as well as the Methodist movement that began to gain momentum after 1774, fed directly into the Revolutionary movement. It did so in two ways. First, Awakened Baptists became eager Patriots during the Revolution. Second, the religious upheaval was "a crisis of authority that prepared the way for the Revolution among both colonial elites and lower orders."[85] Not only did the Awakened Baptists rally their membership for the Patriot cause and raise all-Baptist fighting units during the war, but the Revolution was itself an expression of the same sensibilities that animated the Awakened Baptist revolt. "The two ideologies struck common chords," he said. "Certainly both called for...a world reshaped in truly moral order..." This was a passion that "lay at the heart of both the religious revolution of the evangelicals and the political revolution of the patriots."[86]

Hearts and Minds

I began this discussion by noting how Alexis de Tocqueville thought that the egalitarian "habits of the heart" of Americans, of which religious belief was foremost, most accurately characterized early American democracy. It might seem puzzling, even contradictory, that such a profoundly religious people as those discerned by de Tocqueville should also have

---

[85]Isaac, p. 266.
[86]Isaac, p. 266, 269.

written into their Constitution a separation of church and state. More specifically, the Constitution mandates that there shall be no state establishment of religion. This mandate, however, was not born out of some secular Enlightenment hostility toward religion. Rather, it was born out of the intense religious hostility of Americans toward any manifestations of corrupted religion, toward any manifestations of the Antichrist, of which an established state religion was primary. Even the medieval peasant rebels and early apostolic Christians espoused this same anti-authoritarian sentiment, believing true Christianity was incompatible with hierarchy.

In passing I have also noted the famous belief expressed by John Adams that the Revolution was won in the minds of the people before it was won on the battlefield. What was won in the minds of the people, however, was more than a belief in John Locke's esoteric theories of liberal republicanism. That may have been an expression of their beliefs in a language that Harvard and Yale educated elites were more comfortable in using. But the common folk were perhaps just as much, perhaps more, motivated by what was in their hearts. And this was a deep-rooted belief in the equality of all the faithful in the community of the saints, in the body of Christ Jesus.

In other words, John Locke's ideology of liberal republicanism, which became the dominant political ideology of the new nation, was to a large degree the secular expression of the religious traditions, beliefs, and heritage that Colonial Americans widely shared. American democracy was already religiously embedded in the hearts and minds of ordinary colonial Christians, and had been from the country's genesis, before Patriots won it on Revolutionary battlefields.

Thus, America's dominant political ideology may be formally explicated by pundits and political scientists in the language of John Locke's liberalism, which declares that, for instance, "governments derive their just powers from the consent of the governed."

But it has come to be felt in the hearts and minds of ordinary Americans as a deeply embedded hostility to elites, a belief in general equality, and a belief in, simply put, "power to the people." It is a political stance that is commonly known as populism. And it is the secular expression of a religious impulse that has deep roots in the distant past of Christianity.

It is not likely that any other ideology will soon displace it in the hearts and minds of Americans.

It is the American ideology.

Acknowledgements

For their helpful comments and generous expenditure of time on this work, I would like to thank the following: George Goverman, Anita Alverio, Dr. Van Beck Hall, Dr. Richard Landes, and Dr. Stan Johannesen.

Eric Leif Davin, Ph.D., is the author of *Crucible of Freedom: Workers' Democracy in the Industrial Heartland, 1914-1960; Radicals in Power: The New Left Experience in Office*; *The Great Strike of 1877; The Year of Hope and Fear: Insurrection and Repression, 1919; A Forlorn Hope: Third Parties and American Political Ideology,* and, with Staughton Lynd, *Picket Line and Ballot Box: The Forgotten Legacy of the Labor Party Movement, 1932-1936.*

He is also the author of *The Paterson Strike Pageant: An IWW Novel of Bohemia and Insurgent Labor* and *Solidarity: An IWW Novel of the Steel City.*

His essay, "The Very Last Hurrah: The Defeat of the Labor Party Idea, 1934-1936," appeared in *"We Are All Leaders: The Alternative Unionism of the Early 1930s,"* (University of Illinois Press, 1996), edited by Staughton Lynd. It won the Eugene V. Debs Foundation's prize as the best essay published that year reflecting the enduring spirit of Eugene V. Debs.

www.ingramcontent.com/pod-product-compliance
Ingram Content Group UK Ltd.
Pitfield, Milton Keynes, MK11 3LW, UK
UKHW020234250726
13967UKWH00001B/359

9 781387 482405